ACTION LEARNING FOR MANAGERS

Action Learning for Managers

Mike Pedler

GOWER

© Mike Pedler 2008

Published by
Gower Publishing Limited
Gower House
Croft Road
Aldershot
Hampshire GU11 3HR
England

Gower Publishing Company
Suite 420
101 Cherry Street
Burlington, VT 05401-4405
USA

British Library Cataloguing in Publication Data
Pedler, Mike 1944-
    Action learning for managers
    1. Active learning 2. Executives - Training of
    I. Title
    658.4'07124

    ISBN-13: 978-0566-08863-6

Library of Congress Cataloging-in-Publication Data
Pedler, Mike.
    Action learning for managers / by Mike Pedler.
        p. cm.
    Includes index.
    ISBN 0-566-08863-0
1. Supervisors--Training of. 2. Executives--Training of. 3. Active learning. I. Title.

    HF5549.5.T7P356 2008
    658.4'07124--dc22

2008005473

Printed and bound in Great Britain by TJ International Ltd, Padstow, Cornwall.

Contents

Acknowledgement

I acknowledge the contribution of many people in creating the ideas and materials that form this book. As a powerful approach to personal and organisational development, action learning has been developed over the years by many creative people to produce the methodology with which we work today.

Chief of these is Reg Revans, founder of the idea, who has contributed much to our ideas of what organisational learning might be. To his particular genius and persistence goes the main credit.

This book has its origins in work that I did with John Boutall and others for the National Health Service Training Directorate in 1992. Although the format and contents have been revised and refined several times since then, the aim has remained the same: to be a brief but friendly guide to Revans' action learning.

Introduction

Action learning is an approach to problem solving and learning in groups to bring about change in individuals, teams, organisations and systems. Through action learning people develop themselves and build the relationships that help any system to improve its existing operations and to innovate for the future. Action learning is perhaps the most significant form of personal and organisational development to emerge over the past 30 years.

As a way of working and living, action learning is an vital aspect of the learning organisation. Essentially a simple idea, it requires commitment and care to put into practice.

Action Learning for Managers is designed to:

- provide a practical introduction to action learning that is friendly, lively and encouraging

- help managers and professionals think through the issues they face and how action learning ideas might help them

- offer practice advice on how to promote action learning in your workplace

How to use this book

The guidance in this book is structured around nine key questions – *What is action learning? How does action learning work?* and so on. Each question forms the basis for a chapter with three elements:

- *An explanation* – a response to the title question

- *A case example* – to illustrate the explanation

- *A resource* – a questionnaire, checklist or handout to use in action learning activities

① What is action learning?

In some ways this first question is the most difficult. Reg Revans never gave a one-sentence definition and always maintained that there is no single form or version of action learning. The idea is essentially simple, but, because it is concerned with profound knowledge of oneself and the world, it cannot be communicated as a formula or technique.

Given this proviso, it is possible to describe action learning as it is currently applied in many organisations today. Action learning is an approach to individual and organisational development. Working in small groups known as "sets", people tackle important organisational issues or problems and learn from their attempts to change things.

Action learning has four main elements:

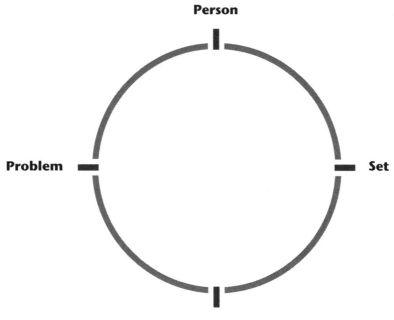

Action on the problem
in the organisation...
and **Learning** from this action

Revans makes the essential point that learning and action require each other:

> *"there is no learning without action and no
> (sober and deliberate) action without learning"*

Action learning brings people together to exchange, support and challenge each other in action and learning. So:

first, each person joins and takes part *voluntarily*. (You can't be sent or send anyone else (though you might work hard at persuading people!);

second, each person must *own* an organisational task, problem or opportunity on which they want to act;

third, because we are much more likely to succeed with the help of friends, *sets* or groups of action learners meet to help each other think through the issues, create options, and above all ...

fourth, take *action and learn* from the effects of that action.

There are many small group initiatives in and around organisations that may well be engaging in action and learning in this way. These include "self-help groups", "support groups", "learning sets", "self-development groups", "productivity improvement meetings", "quality circles" and so on. It is not important what a group is called; the acid test is whether the people concerned are helping each other to take action on their pressing concerns and learning from this work.

This is one of the strengths of action learning. Being *both* profound *and* simple it is never in danger, as mere techniques are, of being here today and gone tomorrow. We always need to re-invent our own ways of putting the basic ideas into practice. This inventing element is what maintains the life in action learning.

It's as simple – and as hard – as that. The only certain way to get a taste for what action learning is like is to do it. However, you can get a better idea of what is involved from listening to others engaged in action and learning. Here is a **case example** which gives a flavour of the life in a set meeting:

CASE EXAMPLE

An action learning set of doctors and managers have been meeting together in a hospital. Don, a consultant physician, is tackling the degree of stress experienced by nurses and other staff in his unit. Here the set members are questioning him about the problem and also wanting to know what has happened since their last meeting:

Don: *Well, it's worse than I thought – our length of stay figures are too high, and the turnover interval is down to less than a day – no wonder everyone rushes around like headless chickens. Morale is low, sickness and absence is way up amongst the nurses and the standard of care is generally too low.*

Shamilla: *It sounds awful, but what about the other figures you were going to bring after the last meeting ... you know, about the types of admissions, the case mix and so on?*

Don: *Ah well ... yes ... this is a bit embarrassing. When I looked at admissions it seems that my senior colleague has far more electives than anyone else – about 40% compared with 10% elsewhere.*

Paul: *So ... what do you make of that?*

Val: *"Research" of course – what else!*

Don: *Er, yes, probably.*

Shamilla: *So, what can you do about it then, Don?*

A discussion follows about possible options for action. At the same time Don is getting a lot of support from his set, who are well aware that this is a delicate situation. No-one tells Don what to do:

Don: (tentatively) Well, I could publish my figures at the next audit meeting ...

Lawrence: What effect would that have?

Don: Well, he might start to argue, but more likely he would just walk out and say my figures are rubbish and I don't know what I'm talking about

Paul: What else could you do? Who else would like to see this issue tackled?

Don: The Chief Executive wants it badly, but I doubt if she'd back me up if it came to it

Lawrence: Have you asked her?

Don: Not exactly ... but you know how it is.

Lawrence: OK I can see the problem, but until you do ask ...

Eventually, and after several more rounds of suggestions and questions, Don decides that the best course of action is to try talking to his senior colleague in private. He'll do this before the next meeting and bring back the results. He looks far from confident. However, with Don having had his turn, the set turns its attention now to Shamilla ...

Taking action in organisations – action of the "sober and deliberate" sort – is often not easy. It may require us to do something different – to "fit out" rather than fit in. There is risk involved in learning in this way; sometimes of incurring the wrath of others, but more often with risking some aspect of ourselves – our reputation or self-image. The learning from such risks can be profound, and the support and challenge of others is important in such circumstances.

The following is a **resource** which gives a more formal definition of action learning and which can be used as a handout.

RESOURCE

What is Action Learning?

Action learning was developed by Revans as the best way to educate managers. It is based on his premise that:

> *"There can be no learning without action and no (sober and deliberate) action without learning."*

Revans suggests that organisations (and the people in them) cannot flourish unless their rate of learning (L) is equal to, or greater than, the rate of change (C) being experienced:

$$L > C$$

Learning has two elements – traditional instruction or *Programmed Knowledge*, and critical reflection or *Questioning Insight*. This gives the learning equation:

$$L = P + Q$$

Revans distinguishes between *puzzles* and *problems*. *Puzzles* have "best" solutions and can be solved via the application of programmed knowledge and with the help of experts. *Problems* have no right answers and are tackled by people in different ways by the exercise of questioning insight. Programmed knowledge can be helpful here but should only be sought after careful reflection on what knowledge is needed and why.

Action learning sets bring people together in order to:

- Work on and through *hitherto intractable problems* of managing and organising. This must be a voluntary commitment.

- Work on problems or opportunities which personally engage the set members – situations in which "I am part of the problem and the problem is part of me".

- Check individual perceptions of the problem, to clarify and render it more manageable, and to create and explore alternatives for action.

- Take action in the light of new insight. This insight begins to change the situation. An account of the effects of the action are brought back to the set for further shared reflection and exploration.

- Provide the balance of support and challenge (*warmth* and *light*) which will enable each member to act and learn effectively.

- Be aware of group processes and develop effective teamwork. Usually sets have an adviser or facilitator whose role is to help members identify and acquire the skills of action and learning.

- Focus on learning at three levels:

  - about the problem or opportunity which is being tackled
  - about what is being learned about oneself
  - about the process of learning itself, ie "learning to learn".

The second and third levels are essential for the transfer of learning to other situations.

(Adapted from the original by Kath Aspinwall)

Cases and handouts like these can be helpful in introducing the idea of action learning, but it is usually best to do this quickly and get on with experimenting with the *experience* of action learning. You can't really teach action learning; but you can set up situations in which people can learn with and from each other through taking action.

There is guidance on how to do this later in the book, but at this point, you might be thinking, "This action learning seems very simple yet powerful; but will it work in my organisation?"

② Will it work in my organisation?

*"Doubt ascending speeds wisdom
from above" (R W Revans)*

Revans' formula for the learning organisation is that good questions flowing upwards help the managers and directors to make good decisions. This is a nice idea. However, as someone once said: "In my company, doubt ascending speeds *retribution* from above"!

So, the first question is: *What sort of organisation is yours*? Is questioning likely to speed wisdom from above or deposit retribution on those below?

In organisations that encourage confident and able people, questioning of work and work processes is a sign of health and fitness. Yet it is a very difficult thing to do where there is no tradition of participation in decisions. In many companies the questioning of senior management decisions is frowned upon or avoided. In these oppressive companies only the brave and/or foolish are up to it. It is "career limiting".

13

In a very efficient, family-owned, department store, the Managing Director was singing the praises of his monthly management meeting. A visitor asked "When where you last questioned on some aspect of company policy?" The MD was astonished: "I can't remember that ever happening", he said. Neither could he see why this might be a desirable thing to happen.

One of action learning's major contributions is the creation of the cultures of enquiry and questioning that are an essential aspect of the learning organisation.

So, the second question is – *Is this what you and your colleagues want?*

Some companies do survive and even prosper with one-way, top-down communications; but those beset by rapid environmental change and increasing competition for markets or resources may find that these constitute serious "learning disabilities" on the part of the organisation. As W Edwards Deming once famously said "survival is not compulsory".

In deciding whether action learning will work in your company, consider the following:

Is there a readiness for action learning?

Does the idea fit with the current stage of development of the organisation? Are people ready to take more initiatives, have more of a say, be entrepreneurial, take risks, run their jobs as if they were their own small businesses? Action learning will not work for an organisation if things are going in the opposite direction.[1]

Do you really want to do it?

It is not for everyone at all times. Organisations which do lots of training do not necessarily welcome action learners. Action learning needs significant organisational problems or opportunities to work on, together with people who are willing to have a go at them. It needs energy and commitment to set it up; have you got enough of this?

Is there support and commitment from the top?

As well as having willing participants with good problems and issues to tackle, action learning is likely to have the biggest impact on individuals and on the organisation when it has support from powerful people:

---

1   Although it might work very well for individuals who can find some space and freedom in the oasis of a set. A friend, who was once the management development manager in a large family-owned and "feudal" organisation, used to organise – unknown to his superiors – sets of people who were fed up with the company. At the first meeting in one set of six, all those present said that they wanted to get out and could the set to help them with their escape plans. After eight or so meetings, two had indeed left the company but the others had all worked on ways of improving their working lives, by moving departments, finding projects and new friends or allies. All this happened in the "shadow side" of the organisation – unknown to and unsanctioned by senior managers.

- Can action learning support their vision and aims for the organisation?

- Does it offer a way forwards on some of *their* problems and issues?

- Will they sponsor change, experiments and the questioning of current practices?

The following **case** illustrates how action learning can flourish where readiness and commitment from the top is apparent:

CASE EXAMPLE

Action learning in John Tann Security Ltd

Colin, John, Les and Pete were senior line managers at John Tann Security Ltd, a heavy metal fabrication company making safes, vaults and security equipment, who formed a management action group with the help of an outside adviser.

The company was faced with a number of problems including small batches, high product variety and changing fashions in the market for security equipment. The directors wanted to increase output and efficiency and also develop the management potential of their key people. Unusually perhaps, they also felt that "often good ideas in a company do not originate at Board level". They wanted to establish an environment in which "ideas would flow upwards through the company structure".

The four managers met weekly with the external adviser over six months and worked well as a team. At the end of this time they reviewed their success together with their sponsoring director. However, and unusually, they did a second review four years later (all of them were still working in the company) and evaluated the benefits under four headings:

1. *Productivity* – from year 1 as a base, the next four years productivity improvements were +11%, +19%, +17% and +13% (the original target was 15%). No one claims that

this stems entirely from the action learning, but this is seen as the major factor.

2. *Individual management development* – the four managers believe that their action learning experience "was the most significant factor" in establishing better decision making, more delegation, less defensive attitudes and improved ability to take criticism, improved self-confidence and leadership, proper application of disciplinary procedures and the ability to confide in their director in the belief that "he wanted them to manage and would allow them to do so".

3. *Team building* – they now operate as a much more effective team.

4. *Continuing use of action learning* – the four formed a set for their deputies and shared the role of adviser in order to pass on what they had learned. This set was not so successful; it met for several meetings but then petered out. The four managers put this down to the presence of one of themselves as part of the company hierarchy and the absence of an external adviser.

Based on Norman Brown "Improving Management Morale and Efficiency" in Pedler MJ (Ed.) *Action learning in Practice*, 2nd Ed, Gower, 1991, pp. 135–146.

John Tann is a good setting for action learning. The participants are keen to have a go, the problems are important and tangible and there is sponsorship from the top. An important value here is the directors' unusual and refreshing belief that the best ideas might not come from themselves. As a result, they welcome the upward flow of ideas. Whilst there are plenty who say they want this, it is not so common to find leaders actually willing to take the risks and to give the power away in this way.

The **resource** in this chapter is an *Organisational Readiness for Action Learning Questionnaire*.

RESOURCE

Organisational Readiness for Action Learning Questionnaire

This will help you assess the chances of success for action learning in your organisation. For each statement score the organisation from 1 (not much like us) to 5 (very like us)

IN THIS ORGANISATION

... people are rewarded for asking good questions
        1 2 3 4 5

... people often come up with new ideas
        1 2 3 4 5

... there is a fairly free flow of communications
        1 2 3 4 5

... conflict is surfaced and dealt with rather than suppressed
        1 2 3 4 5

... we are encouraged to learn new skills
        1 2 3 4 5

... we take time out to reflect on experiences
        1 2 3 4 5

... there are plenty of books, films, packages and other resources for learning

1 2 3 4 5

... people help, encourage and constructively criticise each other

1 2 3 4 5

... we are flexible in our working patterns and used to working on several jobs at once

1 2 3 4 5

... senior people never pull rank and always encourage others to speak their minds

1 2 3 4 5

NOW TOTAL UP YOUR SCORE. IF YOU SCORED ...

... between 10 and 20	Action learning probably won't work in your organisation until things open up a bit more
... 21 to 40	Yes – action learning should work well to help you achieve your purposes
... over 40	You don't need action learning! ... or maybe action learning would help to develop your critical and questioning faculties?

Organisational readiness means being in that situation where action learning offers sufficient challenge to the existing order, yet where there is enough openness and support to give it a chance to thrive.

There are some organisations, especially young, pioneering ones, where action and learning are so uninhibited, so natural and so everyday, that action learning just happens naturally, everyday. People share problems as soon as they see them, they offer help readily and without embarrassment and everybody puts their shoulders to the wheel when necessary. As organisations get older, bigger and more systematic, they can lose this natural action and learning ability. Then action learning can help to loosen things and open people up to innovation.

So, if you have decided that this is right for your organisation, what does an action learning programme look like?

(3) What does an action learning programme look like?

As said at the outset, there is no one, single form for action learning. It might be a group of people meeting at their own initiative or a large organisational programme with many groups linked together in a complex network. An organisational programme will probably have four main components:

Sets

... which work by *meeting* for a full or half day, every four to six weeks, over several months or a year. A facilitator or adviser can help the sets decide on how many meetings to have, where, for how long, when to stop and evaluate and so on. This self-management is an important first step in taking responsibility for our own actions and learning.

Sets need *regular members* who try hard to attend all the meetings. Set meetings focus on members' *problems or tasks* – these form the agenda and the vehicles for action and learning.

Sponsors

... who *support* people in tackling their problems in the organisation and who help them to evaluate the outcomes. Ideally, sponsors are "off line" senior people willing to act as mentors and give their time for the personal and professional development of those involved.

Sponsors may be focused on specific projects or act more as mentors with a broader career or life-centred focus. Some programmes offer mentoring as a separate and additional opportunity. It is important not to offer too much or to clutter the programme with too many roles.

Facilitators

... or advisers, who help things get started, encourage people to share ideas and concerns with each other, and who facilitate the development of the set as a powerful learning system.

The adviser's main concern is with making explicit the learning processes in the set. This helps the members to understand how they, and other people, learn. Of particular importance is the balancing of support and challenge which each of us needs at particular times, and helping the set members to reflect on their learning.

Sets can be self-facilitating. Here people take turns as the facilitator or make sure between them that all these learning process tasks are accomplished. Although most sets start with the help of an external adviser, many go on to become self-facilitating as they acquire the skills and the discipline.

Conferences

... are a good way of linking the action learning sets with the whole system – thereby increasing the likelihood of organisational learning. A conference can be used to start off a programme, and can also be a good place to finish. They are an opportunity to get together, often with senior people, to share with other sets and to report on the action and learning.

In a small printing company, all 50 staff were involved in action learning sets. These groups of four or five were formed by mixing people from the different work processes. Each set picked a joint problem from a list collected by consultants; for example the design of a work process or a relationship with a customer, and were given two hours of company time a week to work on them. At the end of three months, each set met with the owner manager and made presentations. If he approved their proposals (which he did in all cases but one) then the set was then given the responsibility for implementing their plan. At the end of 6 months he hosted a conference with a dinner to celebrate and thank everyone for their efforts.

The following **case** illustrates the structure of an action learning programme in a large engineering company:

CASE EXAMPLE

A design for an action learning programme in an engineering company

Reorganisation had created 36 new teams, and the team leaders took part in the programme with the help of external advisers. Each team leader essentially addressed the same problem: "How do I make this new job/team/structure work?" and although the action and learning on the problem was unique to that person, it was shared in the sets and at the three conferences. The start-up conference included a visit from the MD and Chairman and an introductory activity to give people a taste of action learning and to get them started thinking about their "problems". See the **resource** below for design details of this conference.

The final conference heard evaluation reports from each set and was followed by dinner with the MD and Chairman.

[NB The diagram shows the pattern of the five action learning sets containing the 36 team leaders and the positioning of the 3 conferences]

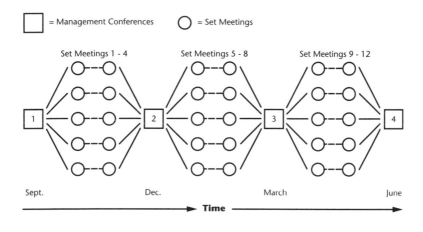

The **resource** is a design for an Action Learning Start-up Conference like the one used in the **case** above. Starting well is always important and it is worth giving people the opportunity to experience what it is like to work in a small group on problems brought by members, as well as having them hear from a leader about why this initiative is important to the organisation.

RESOURCE

Design for a half-day Action Learning Start-up Conference

9:00   Welcome and Introductions

[Programme Manager]

9:30   Where the Company is Going

[Senior Manager]

9:50   What is Action Learning?

[Consultant]

10:10   Activity – "Problems and Questions" (in the whole group)

10:30   Activity – "Working in a Set"

(Split into groups, temporary sets, and work for an hour on some issues raised by members of the group with the help of an adviser. Tea/ coffee taken in these groups)

11:30   Feedback and Questions

[Programme Manager and Consultant]

12:00   Next Steps
                [Programme Manager and Consultant]

        Including:

        1. *Invitation* to join the programme

*NB Action learning only works with volunteers who <u>want</u>
to act and learn by tackling a problem. It should be made
as comfortable as possible <u>not</u> to join where there are good
reasons, e.g. personal or being part of a similar programme
elsewhere.*

                2. If you decide to join – then the *next steps*
                    are (i) to inform the Programme Manager
                    (ii) discuss the programme and your
                    "problem" with your manager, sponsor,
                    mentor; (iii) prepare an initial statement of
                    your problem as you see it.

12:30   <u>Close</u>

After this "taster" session some unofficial work behind the scenes may be necessary to get the action learning started. People may wish to talk through concerns before making the decision to join, such as what sort of "problems" or "opportunities" they can discuss. Some managers may need encouragement to give their people the proper permission to take part. Do whatever it takes to get the sets off to a good start.

For example, it is worth considering whether to allow the temporary groups from the start-up conference to continue if they wish to do so. If the day has gone well for a particular group they may just want to get on with it. The only sensible thing to do with that sort of energy is to get out of the way.

Once started, how does an action learning set work?

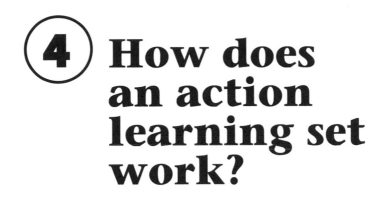

4 **How does an action learning set work?**

At the first meeting, the facilitator will encourage people to introduce themselves, to explore what each wants to do and learn and to discuss ground rules for working together.

The first meeting should allow time for each person to describe the problem or issue that they have brought with them. If a person is clear about what needs doing and what they want to do, that's fine, the set can get on and help as best they can. However, a person's concerns may be tentative or unformed, and this is no bad thing at this stage; a sincere question which begins with "How can I ...?" is a very good starting place for action and learning.

Although all sets develop differently and create their own patterns and practices, a popular format for subsequent meetings is:

* *Catching-up* – a round which allows each person to share immediate news and helps to re-integrate the group

- *Agenda setting* – based on what they have heard in the catch up round, members set the agenda, decide on a "batting order" and allocate the available time. In principle everyone has equal time but this may be varied depending on need, urgency and so on.

- *Progress reports* – each person takes it in turn to report on progress since the last meeting and where they are now. The other set members help the person learn from what has happened and explore options for new directions and actions. They do this by keeping the focus on the person and their problem, questioning, supporting, challenging and offering help of various sorts.

- *Review* – at the end of each session, the set takes a few minutes for feedback and discussion of the process – "What worked well?" "What was difficult in this meeting?" "How could we be more effective?"

It is often a mistake to try to get down to business too early, especially if it some time since the set has met. Good sets take special care to bring everyone in at the start of a meeting, making sure that all are "here" and remembering what you talked about last time and in full attention. Twenty minutes work in a focused group can be worth an hour or more in one which is not concentrating collectively.

Some important processes in sets include:

- People **presenting** their views or perceptions of the problem or opportunity they are tackling. This involves possibly confidential information about their organisations and colleagues and also self-disclosure of feelings, fears, hopes, limitations, strengths and so on. To do this work, sets need ...

- **Ground rules** to govern behaviour inside and outside the set. One example might be that all members have an equal right to the time and attention of the set. Another might be that people cannot discuss "set business" outside. Good ground rules help with ...

- **Supporting** people in their attempts at understanding, action and learning. Over time a good set builds its capability in offering both support and challenge to people's existing views and positions. A strong sense of support ("Warmth") helps to enable the quality of challenge ("Light") in the set. Challenges come especially through ...

- **Questioning** in response to members' presentations and "status reports". The aim is to find those questions that help the person *question themselves*, especially on aspects which they may not have previously considered. This is the process that can lead to Q or "questioning insight". As sets mature, they improve in their ability to support and challenge. It takes time, consistent membership and regular meetings to develop a good ...

- **Set development process** whereby the set forms, develops working practices and learns to operate creatively and productively. Having got to know and tested each other, people begin to create a strong joint commitment.

In a mature set there is a collective sense of being "all for one and one for all" – where all take pleasure from any person's small "victory" or when the penny drops for someone and they get a new insight into their situation. The set process is developed by regular ...

- **Reviews**, in which people stop work and reflect on how well the set as a whole is working. "How effective are we in helping each other act and learn?"

Facilitation and *evaluation* are other key processes in sets, and are dealt with in later chapters.

The following **case** demonstrates the questioning process in an action learning set.

CASE EXAMPLE

On a management development programme in an airline, an early set meeting is rather frantic and busy, with people cutting each other off and not listening well. The external facilitator reflects this back to the set and suggests a way to improve the group process:

Facilitator: *Let's start with Carol; can you summarise your situation in one or two sentences, please? Everyone else concentrate on listening, don't speak but instead write down any thoughts or questions you have.*

Carol: *It comes down to my agreeing with my boss to try to improve relationships with some of our suppliers. We have quality and delivery problems with some and I think we also have too many of them. However, people are very committed to their particular contacts. I could easily rationalise things but it's important to keep good relationships all round ... is that enough to start with?*

Facilitator: *Yes, I think so, thanks Carol. OK, now an interesting thing about working in action learning sets is that you find out how differently people see things. Could everyone please offer Carol a question? So if you have made an observation, perhaps you could turn it into a question? Before we start, Carol, please don't try to answer these now, just listen and write down word for word what people say.*

In ten minutes the other six set members offer nineteen questions for Carol to write down, including:

> How many suppliers do you have now?
> Have you spoken to any suppliers?
> Have you quantified the costs of poor quality, late deliveries etc.?
> What's the history? How long has it been like this?
> You talk about what the boss wants – what do you want?
> What's in it for your boss?
> Who else – apart from you and the boss – thinks this is a problem?
> What's your relationship like with your boss?
> How do your colleagues feel about the situation?
> How have your colleagues got to behave differently?
> Whose side are you on?
> What have you got to gain from acting on this?
> Why change? What are the benefits?

Facilitator: *OK, thanks ... good questions. Carol, which of these questions do you want to pursue? Which are most interesting to you?*

Carol: *They are all good questions, but the ones I hadn't really thought about are what I want for myself and Max's about whose side am I on ... what do you mean by whose side am I on?*

The set then continues with Carol back in charge of her time ...

This is just one glimpse of a set at work. Sets come with many differences depending on the individuals in them and the organisational cultures to which they belong. The basic operational guidelines for a set are worth formalising as ground rules. The **resource** for this chapter gives an example of ground rules for a set.

RESOURCE

Ground Rules for Action Learning

Each set should establish its own ground rules and can operate to any rules upon which members agree. Discussion should take place at the first meeting and the resulting rules should be revisited at the second meeting and at review sessions to check on their continuing appropriateness and effectiveness. Some important ground rules shared by many sets are:

- **Confidentiality** – matters discussed in the set are not to be taken outside

  [Confidentiality is often first on a group's list, but what does it mean? Can I talk about *my* action, thoughts, feelings etc. to other people? Can I disclose this particular thing to my partner or mentor? "Confidentiality" needs clarification in most sets.]

- **Commitment** to attending and having a really good reason if you can't

- Everyone has a right to their **time** – but they don't have to take it

---

- Everyone should be **listened** to

- We agree to offer each other **support and challenge** but avoid judgements

- It is safe here to admit **needs, weaknesses and mistakes**

- **Punctuality** – we should start and finish on time

Some other ground rules I've seen are:

- Meetings rotate around each person's workplace

- Each meeting starts with bids for time

- At each session, part of the time is given to members sharing their special knowledge

- Two's and three's meeting separately outside the set is OK

- Sub-groups meeting separately outside the set is NOT OK

- The facilitator should have some time in the set for his/her issues

- Achievements will be celebrated in an appropriate way

- Members should keep a log book of progress on their problem

- Set meetings can be at members' homes

Having got the set off to a good start, what about the issues or problems that people bring? What makes a good problem or opportunity for action learning?

(5) What is an action learning problem?

An action learning *problem* is an issue, a concern, an opportunity or a task that you want to *do* something about. Revans' use of this word causes difficulties for some people, perhaps because they associate it with personal problems, not for public consumption.

For Revans, the problem is the starting place for enquiry and action. He makes the distinction between problem and puzzle. *Puzzles* may look like problems but in fact are "right answer" situations where solutions already exist. There are no single right responses to *problems*, but through action you can learn to change the situation.

Being unable to start your car is a problem for you, but it's really a puzzle – there is someone out there, an expert with special knowledge, who knows how to resolve this. Getting my colleague to change the way he works in relation to me is a true problem in the action learning sense: this is a situation where there is no right answer (despite what the "Hero Manager" books say).

An action learning *problem* is a vehicle for learning which requires us to come up with ideas for action, to try them out and then to reflect on that to see what we have learned. In this way we learn about the problem itself *and* about ourselves, the way we think, act, and relate to others. This learning not only moves us forwards in this particular situation, but also helps with how we work on *all* problems.

The following **case** illustrates the different sorts of problems that people can work on in action learning sets:

CASE EXAMPLE

An action learning set in Hallam City Council

The first meeting of a Hallam City Council action learning set revealed three different kinds of problem:

Maya's problem was focused and specific. She had a graduate trainee on a 6-month attachment and had agreed to mentor him, but felt that he was not fitting in well. At first she had given him the benefit of the doubt and, anyway, she was just too busy. Now she had received one or two complaints about work quality to add to the various odd comments she had heard. Maya felt she should do something about it. She was concerned that she had not lived up to her promise and her own expectations and that she was letting down both the trainee and her department. How should she tackle the problem?

The facilitator observed that this clear-cut problem made it easy for members to focus their attention and come up with options for action. However, there could be deeper issues underlying this apparently simplicity.

Roy's problem was different. When he joined his present department he had been promised that he would be able to develop an area of work of great personal and professional interest; tenant participation in decisions about housing management and maintenance. However, since starting the job he had got precisely nowhere and was beginning to feel

43

that his boss was not so much not interested in the work as actively opposed. Fed up with this, he doesn't know whether to push this or whether to explore other ways of making a start. He wonders aloud whether race comes into it; Roy is black (as are many of his tenants), his boss is white.

The facilitator acknowledges Roy's feelings and concerns and notes that this is a very different problem from Maya's. The options for action are less straightforward and hedged around with sensitivities. This problem will not resolve easily although there is a great potential here for learning from "sober and deliberate" action.

Kieron's problem is different again. His department is an unhappy place. The old manager who had run the department for 22 years had recently retired on ill health grounds after having been accused of impropriety over the use of official funds and equipment. The threat of a review is hanging over everyone and the old deputy – now the new acting manager – is identified with the old boss. As a team leader, Kieron accepts that many procedures had been rather casual, but at least everyone knew where they were before; now all was at sea. The department is under great pressure as a result of external competition and is likely lose work and therefore jobs. Kieron summed it up: "We just haven't got our act together."

The facilitator remarks that some problems are just too big and overwhelming. For Kieron's sake, and also for the others in the set, it might be better to choose something more local and specific. She asks Kieron to begin by describing his own team ...

These are very different sorts of problem, but they have two things in common: they are all amenable to action and learning; and they all have both personal and organisational aspects.

This is true of all "problems" worthy of the name. Whoever tackles a problem must have a sense of personal ownership of it – she or he must want to do something about it – otherwise there will be no action and learning. But an action learning problem is more than just personal; it affects other people in other places who will have views about it and their own personal stakes in it.

Action (including thinking, exploring, rehearsing and actually doing) has two aspects: *inside* me and *outside* on the problem in the organisation; learning is similarly *both* about the outside problem *and* about me:

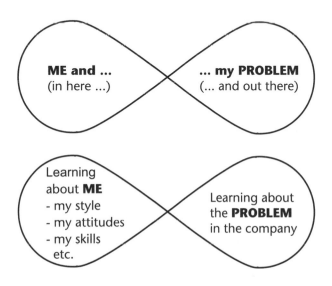

Giving it a good go

This issue of personal commitment is crucial. A shrewd manager once explained to me that he had encouraged an experienced shopfloor worker to join a managerial action learning programme because "he would give it a good go". This has been one of my acid tests ever since.

The **resource** for this chapter offers some questions to help you think through a suitable problem for action learning.

RESOURCE

Action Learning Problem Brief

These questions will help you to think through a suitable problem, opportunity or issue for action learning:

1. Describe your problem situation in one sentence:

2. Why is this important?

    (i) To you?
    (ii) To your company?

3. How will you recognise progress on this problem?

4. Who else would like to see progress on this problem?

5. What difficulties do you anticipate?

6. What are the benefits if this problem is reduced or resolved?

    (i)   To me?
    (ii) To other people?
    (iii) To the organisation?

In the John Tann case (Chapter 2), the set members had very clear ideas about what they wanted to do. It is often harder than this to define problems tightly enough so as to arrive at clear, measurable outcomes or success criteria. NB: this is no reason not to try.

Sometimes it is easier to develop a picture or vision of how things could be different. People may be able to draw a picture or tell a story of what things would be like if they were different and better around here in this respect. Where measurable outcomes are just not possible, we can sometimes draw or describe changed attitudes, better relationships or shared understanding. See Chapter 8 for an example of a drawing that helped in this way.

Having defined, and probably redefined, some good problems; what are the skills which set members need to develop and demonstrate?

(6) What skills are developed in action learning?

Many valuable skills are developed through practising action learning. There are three key roles in the action learning set; each of which develops particular abilities:

- *Presenting* a problem

- *Helping* others with their problems, and

- *Facilitating* the process

Some of the skills and abilities which can be learned in these roles are:

1. *Presenting* a problem

    - taking and holding the focus of the set
    - analysing and describing a problem
    - asking for help, advice, assistance

- being able to receive – help, advice, feedback, challenge
- ability to reflect on what you receive and experience
- staying in charge of your time, problem, learning
- planning next steps
- proactivity (a tendency to initiate action)
- skills in organisational politics
- resilience and perseverance
- self-belief

2. *Helping* others with their problems

   - belief in others (in their ability to understand the world in their way, take action on their problem etc.)
   - empathy
   - credulous listening (ability to listen to others and suspend your own evaluations)
   - ability to give – help, advice, assistance
   - questioning
   - supporting
   - challenging
   - generating options for action
   - willingness to support outside the set

3. *Facilitating* the process

   - facilitating members' giving to and receiving from each other
   - ability to summarise and draw the 'big picture'

- understanding of learning processes in individuals, groups and organisations
- understanding of the micro-politics of the organisation
- ability to question self and admit uncertainties and errors

All of these skills might broadly be defined as *learning skills* (though some are more tendencies, abilities or qualities). Their purpose is to help people move round the action and learning cycle:

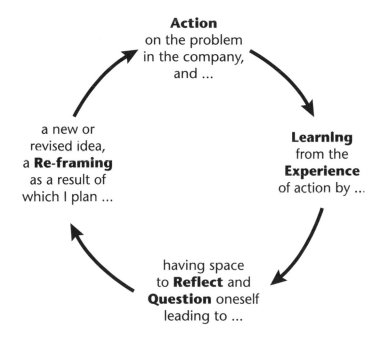

Action
on the problem
in the company,
and ...

Learning
from the
Experience
of action by ...

having space
to **Reflect** and
Question oneself
leading to ...

a new or
revised idea,
a **Re-framing**
as a result of
which I plan ...

The following **case** gives some examples of what people have learned from working in sets:

CASE EXAMPLE

What individuals have learned from action learning

The following comments, taken from various reviews and evaluations, give a sense of what can be learned in action learning:

One manager learned a lot about how to make things happen:

> *"I knew what had to be done after a couple of sessions in the set – the problem was how to do it? I was keen but no one else seemed to be bothered. I was encouraged by the set to go around and talk to people who might be interested. For a while nothing much seemed to happen and then it was as if everyone thought it was a good idea! There was actually no resistance there, it was just me, imagining it ..."*

A director also found that she was part of the problem:

> *"When I joined the set I was very clear about my problem and I simply expected the others to give me the benefit of their experience and more or less tell me what they thought I should do. To some extent this happened but what I hadn't expected was that I would be pushed and prodded and encouraged to really think through my problem for myself. What I learned was that this issue was as much to do with me and the way I operate as a Finance Director as it was to do with the apparent practical blockage which was bugging me, my boss and the others in the department."*

Another manager learned the valuable skill of questioning:

> *"You can try to teach individuals, but only they can learn. I am probably now well known for my questioning approach to resolving issues!"*

Whilst this person discovered that everything in the company seemed to be connected:

> *"I started off trying to introduce some rationality into the queueing system for orders, but as I progressed through the company – with a lot of encouragement from my boss and from the CEO – I realised that what was wrong was the whole way we were organised. In the terms I've learned since being here, we needed to be less of a hierarchy and more of a lateral flow from buyer to supplier and back to buyer. So what we have is a major change instead of a minor one – much of it is being done by other people of course – but it's been very exciting being the cause of it all."*

In another account the crucial role of top management is made clear:

> *"The biggest theme for me is the impact of top managers. If the person at the top is learning something new for themselves, then the whole organisation is healthier. Sadly, it seems to me that the evidence from this project is more negative than positive. Top managers seem to be lonely figures, struggling with huge agendas, often continuing to get involved in day-to-day operational issues, anxious and*

stressed about personal futures and not appearing to be using personal support or learning processes to any great extent."

Commonly, people learn much about the learning process itself:

"There is a sudden moment when learning happens ... I had been in turmoil ... unable to come to terms with the problem facing me. I didn't want the change and I couldn't talk to anybody. I was under stress – being disagreeable, wallowing in self-pity, arguing the toss with myself. I decided to speak to the one person who could help and woke up that morning thinking 'this is action learning in practice'. Of course, that person couldn't help me, but the conversation wasn't futile because I suddenly realised that this was my problem – that only I could do something about it. This seems to me to be the quintessential moment – when you decide to own the problem and not make it someone else's fault that you have the problem."

and

"We didn't all learn the same things or at the same time – the penny dropped for us at different times – and some people learned more and others seemed to benefit less."

One person had adopted the action learning approach in many aspects of her life:

"Action learning has become more like a philosophy to me, something I use in all my activities. I challenge myself all the time, why? For what reason? Be positive! There is an answer! I have also suffered pain, emotionally,

going through change myself with the organisation. We cannot be divorced from it, if we affect it, it must affect us, touch us."

Whilst these skills, abilities and qualities will help everyone with action and learning, they are not the most critical element. Skilled performance is almost always preferable to unskilled, but the first essential in action learning is the desire and willingness to act and learn.

When learning, you can't be skilful all of the time: being incompetent is part of the process. You don't need to be fully skilled to do action learning; the key question is: *Are you willing to give it a go?*

The **resource** below gives some useful ideas for questioning – the first and primary skill of action learning:

RESOURCE

Good questions for action learning

Revans' three key questions:

Who knows ... about the problem?

Who cares ... about the problem? and

Who can ... do anything about the problem?

are more than enough to get started, referring as they do to the three central processes in human action – thinking, feeling and willing. Much management education focuses upon just one of these – thinking – do you understand the problem? Have you analysed it correctly?

But how you *feel* about your situation and how much commitment or *will* you have to act, are just as vital – maybe even more so. Well-educated people in particular may be liable to getting stuck at the thinking stage, or paralysis by analysis, where planning never leads to action.

Useful questions for action and learning are:

What am I trying to do?

What is stopping me from doing it?

What can I do about it?

Who knows what I am trying to do?

Who cares about what I'm trying to do?

Who else can do anything to help?

Some other questions which may facilitate work in the set are:

- What do you want to get out of this session?

- Can you tell us the story as it happened?

- What have you learned from that?

- What do you most need from us now?

- How do other people in the situation – colleagues, friends, partner, boss etc. feel about this?

- How do you feel about what is going on?

- What questions does that raise?

- How can we help you move forwards on this issue?

- How would someone you most admire deal with this situation?

- Can you think of three options for action?

- What are the pros and cons of each of these options?

- What first steps are you going to take before our next meeting?

- On a scale of 1 to 10, how likely are you to do this action?

and

- How can we make this set more effective?

The adviser or facilitator will usually model such questions, but anyone can acquire this valuable skill. The more capable you are with the various action learning skills, the more likely it is that you will want to have a go at self-facilitating your set, with members taking on the role in turn or carrying it out collectively.

One question that is nearly always raised about action learning concerns evaluation. How do we know that action learning is worthwhile?

(7) How do you evaluate action learning?

To evaluate means to place a value upon something. Value is judged against certain criteria and the more specific these are, the easier it is to determine value.

You can evaluate for two purposes, for:

- *Development* – to make things better, to improve action and learning

or for

- *Judgement* – to assess the impact or contribution of something.

Developmental evaluation ought to be part of the on going life of any set, and the **resource** in this section provides a simple form for reviewing a set meeting for the purpose of improving action and learning.

Judgemental evaluation is important to establish whether goals have been met and resources well used. It is generally good practice to encourage people to think about their "success criteria" in the action learning set. Where specific criteria can be set, results can be compared against the targets.

Although evaluation is a critical activity and should be planned in from the outset, it can be a struggle to keep it simple and efficient. It is easiest to assess the effects of something close up "the set seemed to work well today" or "I learned so much this morning". But to answer a question like: "What is the total value of the action and learning?" you have to look at the effects not only on the tasks but ultimately on the organisation as a whole.

The work of an action learning set can be evaluated at several levels:

- *Individual* – in terms of progress on a problem and the learning from it

- *Set* – in terms of group development, maturity and collective achievement

- *Programme or whole organisation level* – across the sets, impact on the whole

You can also evaluate at different points in time, for example:

- *Immediate outcome* – for example, at the end of set meeting (see **resource**)

- *Intermediate outcome* – for example, half way through a programme or series of meetings

- *Programme outcome* – at the end of the set or programme

- *Organisational outcome* – long enough after the set or programme to gauge the effects on the company

In terms of judgemental evaluation, it is difficult to ascribe cause and effect at the whole organisation level. How do we know that the action learning set or programme reduced costs by 23 per cent – when there were so many other factors at work? Often, the best we can do here is to get people's judgements on this – as in the John Tann case in Chapter 2. In the case of such qualitative data, it is useful to collect judgements from a range of the stakeholders to any problem.

The following **case** shows how to identify these stakeholders, together with their success criteria for an action learning programme in a school system:

CASE EXAMPLE

An action learning set for headteachers and deputies

An action learning set of headteachers and deputies identified a range of internal and external stakeholders for each school:

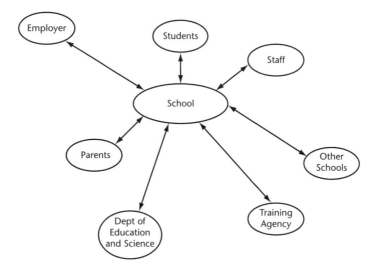

Each set member used the stakeholder map to identify the critical success criteria for their personal projects. For example, one deputy head wanted to improve the delivery of aspects of the National Curriculum:

Stakeholder	Success Criteria	Evidence Needed
1. Students	(i) "more interesting lessons" (ii) "to know what is expected in terms of assessment" etc.	(i) End of term lesson reviews (ii) Improved achievements
2. Parents	(i) "to know how their child is doing" (ii) "to know how to help their child do well" etc.	(i) Feedback on reports and open evenings (ii) Access to after-school information sessions etc.
3. Department of Education and Science etc.		

The set carried out a rigorous final evaluation, visiting each other's schools to check progress on how far the various stakeholders' criteria had been met. A report noted these examples:

● Staff in one school reported that: "Relationships between the school and parents have improved dramatically. Attendances at open evenings have doubled and parents report feeling more confident in terms of asking for information."

● A headteacher said: "It helped me a lot – I used to get very stressed and had a bad relationship with my deputy – now our ability to communicate and work together has improved. I feel better and I think the school does too."

● Several set members said they had picked up all sorts of tools and techniques from other members which they had put into practice in their schools.

- A Chairman of Governors interviewed by two members of the set said that she and the other governors had noticed the school seemed "to be running more smoothly and that there was less of an air of crisis".

- Various improvements in performance and achievements were observed in the schools.

- One deputy said of the action learning set: "It was an oasis ... sheer bliss to get away from the school for half a day and have people actually listen to you! Also to listen to yourself ... and to hear how other people were tackling their problems."

Self-evaluation is an important part of action learning. Self-awareness and improving one's ability to self-evaluate is an important outcome in itself.

Carrying out a more formal judgemental evaluation, for example, interviewing stakeholders and assessing how far their expectations have been met can be a good last task for an action learning set – as in the **case** above. Such a collective review of work and learning can be an excellent way to "make a good end".

The minimum specification for evaluation is twofold. First, a regular review for developmental evaluation in set meetings. Second, a summary, judgemental evaluation of the worth of the programme as a whole to the individuals and organisations concerned.

The **resource** for this chapter is a Set Meeting Review Worksheet, which may be especially useful in the early stages of a set to embed the habit of evaluation:

RESOURCE

Set Meeting Review Worksheet

Each person should spend 5 minutes reflecting individually on the work of the set and before sharing their thoughts with fellow members on:

1. **MY PROBLEM** The three key things I have learned about my problem today are:

   •

   •

   •

2. **MYSELF** The one thing I've learned about myself today is:

---

3. **ACTION** My action steps before the next meeting are:

   ●

   ●

   ●

4. **OTHER SET MEMBERS** The most interesting thing I have learned today about the problems facing each of the other set members is:

   Name:

   Name:

   Name:

   Name:

   Name:

5. **THE SET** The thing that stands out for me today in terms of the working of this set is:

Through action learning we can achieve impressive results for both individuals and organisations. Yet it is important to bear in mind that action learning is no panacea or miracle cure. I have tried to point out some likely pitfalls throughout, whilst at the same time trying to encourage you to get on with it. Please do this, and then read Chapter 8 when you're ready to reflect on the method itself.

(8) Surely action learning can't do everything?

No, of course it can't. Some of the chief limitations of action learning have been spelled out earlier, especially in Chapter 2. Conditions have to be right for action learning, there has to be a readiness – in individuals and in companies – or it will not take hold. In all the action learning projects that I have worked on, some sets have worked and contributed better than others; and whilst many people have derived great benefit, some – usually a small minority – find that it didn't work for them.

If your purpose is to train individuals in specific skills or knowledge, then there are probably more efficient and effective ways of doing this. If your purpose is to make a shift in the organisation or system, then action learning can certainly play an important part. But it can't do the whole job on its own; also required here are a new vision, leadership from the top, specific resource commitments and so on.

71

Action learning is first and foremost an *idea* or philosophy and not simply an alternative educational or training method. Revans sought to heal the split that he saw as having developed historically between thinking and doing, ideas and action. In presenting action and learning as parts of each other, he aimed to contribute to the resolution and improvement of the many urgent and pressing problems facing our society. In particular he was concerned with those not able to help themselves – which includes all of us from time to time – and once described the essence of action learning as "helping each other help the helpless".

Revans is a radical whose writings make clear that he intends action learning to be a deeper, more revolutionary process than just a training method for "learning by doing". Action learning contains a *moral philosophy* concerning individual and social development and involving:

- **Honesty about self** – the most valuable question learned by the managers on his Belgian programme was "What is an honest man, and what do I need to do to become one?"

- **Attempting to do good in the world** – Revans' quotes both St James – "be ye doers of the word, and not only hearers of it" and Shaw's echo, in *Back to Methuselah*, "It is not enough to know what is good; you must be able to do it".

- **For the purpose of friendship** – "All meaningful knowledge is for the sake of action, and all meaningful action for the sake of friendship" (John Macmurray *The Self as Agent*) – a key text for Revans.

Many people across the world have learned the value of action learning without ever having heard of Revans or his philosophy. This is because action learning does offer a very practical form of managerial self-help. As one manager put it:

> *"the group format provides rare 'space' in organisational life; a time for reflection and review; a way of linking individual and collective learning; permission to be completely open in a confidential setting; and support, challenge and encouragement. These features allow learning both about management and, at a deeper level, about oneself as a manager."*

This space and opportunity is created by the application of the action learning idea; the method if you like. However, the method derives its vitality from the underlying philosophy above; and the outcome is both very practical and somewhat mysterious and profound.

The following **case** illustrates the practical value of action learning through the work of Tony, a hospital doctor, who is angry about his organisation and who wants to change it. As well as being angry, he feels powerless, impotent.

CASE EXAMPLE

The angry doctor

Tony is a psychiatrist in a large NHS Mental Health Trust. He is angry a lot of the time – about the changes to the NHS, the pressures on him, the service offered to his patients, the attitude of managers who always seem to want more for less and offer little in the way of help. There's a lot to be angry about. Yet this anger actually doesn't help him to get what he wants.

The facilitator stops Tony in the middle of one of his rants and suggests that he take 10 or 15 minutes to draw the situation as he experiences it. After a short argument, Tony goes off with a pen and a flipchart to another room. He returns with this picture:

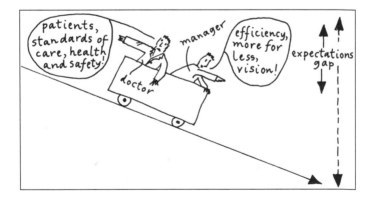

The Facilitator asks Tony

"How does it feel for each of the people in the picture?"

... which leads to an interesting discussion about the feelings of the manager in the picture. Two key questions and a proposal emerge in the next 20 minutes

"What does the picture tell us about the relationship of the doctor and the manager?"

(The most obvious thing being – to one set member at least – is that that the two have their backs to each other...)

"What is stopping movement on this problem?"

As Tony's time runs out, the facilitator makes a proposal:

"Can you come back next time having given some thought to the 'I – WE – THEY' actions?

What do I need to do?

What do WE need to do? and

What do THEY need to do? that is those people not in the picture."

Tony agrees to go and think about these questions, talk to a few people and report back next time.

Through breaking away from words for a time, Tony manages to look at himself and his situation from a different perspective, and perhaps with a bit more honesty about his own contribution. This does not mean that he is wrong to be angry. But whilst anger is a sound feeling in the face of injustice and unfairness, it is often a bad guide to action. The aim here is to find possibilities for action and learning that might improve everyone's health.

This example shows how drawing problems can often help people get a clearer perspective. Professionals and managers who deal mainly in words, also easily get lost in them. We become used to using words to hide things as well as to explain them. Sometimes we don't even know when we are doing this. Drawing the situation gets away from the words and creates clarity, honesty, openness.

Revans is always on the side of the individual seeking to act and learn, but he is also concerned to specify the conditions that should best promote action learning. This is his vision of the learning organisation:

RESOURCE

Revans on the Learning Organisation

Reg Revans makes it clear that action learning is not just about individual learning in small groups. His "upward communication of doubt" holds the record for the shortest definition of the learning organisation. In *The Enterprise as a Learning System* (1969) he describes how this is to be achieved:

- "that its chief executive places high amongst his own responsibilities that for developing the enterprise as a learning system; this he will achieve through his personal relations with his immediate subordinates, since the conduct of one level of a system towards any level below it is powerfully influenced by the perception that the higher level has of its own treatment from above...

- ... the maximum authority for subordinates to act... *become known by interrogation from below...*

- ... codes of practice, standard rules and procedures, works orders and other such regulations are to be seen as norms around which variations are deliberately encouraged as learning opportunities...

- any reference of what appears to be an intractable problem to a superior level should be accompanied by *both* an explanation of why it cannot be treated where it seems to have arisen *and* a proposal to change the system so that similar problems arising in future could be suitably contained and treated;

- persons at all levels should be encouraged, with their immediate colleagues, to make regular proposals for the study and reorganisation of their own systems of work;"

Source: Revans R.W., "The Enterprise as a Learning System" in Pedler, M. (ed.) (1997) *Action Learning in Practice*, 3rd ed. Aldershot, UK: Gower.

$\textcircled{9}$ Where can I get more help?

As you've no doubt gathered by now, there's really only one way to get going with action learning and that is to try it. If you've read this far then you're interested enough to have a go; so, take some (sober and deliberate) action and you will learn.

Some final words, please *don't*:

- try to structure things too much – aim for the minimum critical specification

- control the life out of the idea

- follow all the advice in this guide!

It will almost certainly help if you *do*:

- recruit some good friends and allies to work with you

- choose some of the most intractable and interesting problems around to work with

- make the time to reflect on and learn from your actions; keep a journal, carry out reviews and evaluations.

Some further resources are given below. Here are some starting points on networks, journals, guides and other useful books:

Networks

IFAL (The International Foundation for Action Learning) provides an advisory service, publishes a newsletter, maintains a useful library and a bibliography service, holds workshops, and otherwise disseminates information about action learning. Membership is open to individuals and organisations; details from:

Pam Wright
IFAL Administrator
c/o Department of Management Learning
The University of Lancaster
LANCASTER
LA1 4YX
UK

Tel: 01524 720115
e-mail: p.wright@lancaster.ac.uk
www.ifal.org.uk

IFAL has a number of international affiliations, including:

IFAL USA	www.ifal-usa.org
IFAL Netherlands	www.actionlearning.nl
IFAL Sweden	www.cfal.se

Journals

Action Learning: Research & Practice is an international journal dedicated to the advancement of knowledge and practice through action learning. It publishes academic papers, practitioner "accounts of practice" and reviews. Details from:

Helen James
Journal Administrator, Action Learning: Research & Practice
Henley Management College
Greenlands
Henley on Thames
Oxon.
RG9
UK

Tel: 01491 571454
e-mail: Helen.James@henleymc.ac.uk
http://www.tandf.co.uk/journals/titles/14767333.asp

Guides

A user-friendly guide to action learning especially written for people who want to facilitate themselves is:

D-I-Y Handbook for Action Learners (2005) Mandy Chivers and Mike Pedler Liverpool: Merseycare NHS Trust

Available from:

Mandy Chivers
Merseycare NHS Trust
Parkbourn
Maghull
Merseyside
L31 1HW

Tel: 0151 473 0303
e-mail: Mandy.Chivers@merseycare.nhs.uk

Books

Reg Revans has written eloquently over many years about action learning. His books repay repeated study but unfortunately all are now out of print and must be had from libraries, including IFAL's, or second-hand. Four key books are:

- *ABC of Action Learning* (1998) London: Lemos & Crane.

Revans attempt to spell out the idea as simply as possible. His shortest book but solidly packed.

- *The Origins and Growth of Action Learning* (1982) Bromley, Kent: Chartwell-Bratt.

The "collected works" – over 50 papers extending from 1945 to 1981.

- *Developing Effective Managers* (1971) New York: Praeger.

Revans' most significant attempt to develop the theory and practice of action learning based on a Belgian programme that swapped top managers between companies and industries.

- *Action Learning: New Techniques for Managers* (1980) London: Blond and Briggs.

A review of Revans' action learning practice around the world.

There are also an increasing number of books on action learning by other authors. Two books that I have found useful are:

McGill, I. and Beaty, L. (2000) *Action Learning: A Practitioner's Guide*, Second Edition, London: Kogan Page.

A lively and readable book that is good on the skills involved in action learning.

Weinstein, K. (1999) *Action Learning: A Journey in Discovery and Development*, Aldershot UK: Gower Publishing Company Ltd.

A good read, distinguished by its giving voice to action learning participants rather than pundits.

Index

**If you have found this book
useful you may be interested
in other titles from Gower**

www.gowerpub.com

**59 Checklists for Project and
Programme Management
Second Edition**
Rudy Kor and Gert Wijnen
978-0-566-08775-2

Critical Chain
Eliyahu M Goldratt
978-0-566-08038-8

**Essentials of Project Management, The
Third Edition**
Dennis Lock
978-0-566-08805-6

GOWER

.